You don't need permission to be powerful:
Finding it for yourself

✣

Cassy Dinius, MA
Tamara Dinius

Art by: Tamara dinius

The world awaits!

Bravely follow your heart... It knows where to go!

We spent many hours reading, learning, writing, editing, and creating so that you could hold this book in your hands. Please do not reproduce, distribute, or transmit this publication in any form or by any means without our prior written permission. This includes electronic or mechanical methods such as photocopying.

You can contact us at:
CJDinius@gmail.com
TJDinius@gmail.com
www.womenwineandwords.com

Copyright © 2018 Cassy Dinius, Tamara Dinius
All rights reserved.
ISBN:9781976520730

DEDICATION

To everyone with a story they hold inside: in this book, I share my truth so that one day you may share yours.

When others are brave enough to be vulnerable, I grow. Their honesty gives me reassurance and affirmation so that I can be strong too.

Art unites us in ways that words cannot. It allows communication and understanding between strangers. Art can connect us, empower us, inspire us. It reminds us, "You are not alone."

I dedicate this book to those who have shared their stories with me. You have inspired me to reach further and dig deeper. I create art because it's in me to do so, I share it in hopes that it makes a difference.

YOUR STORIES

A woman purchased a piece of art with the words *I can and I will...just watch me*. She bought the largest one I had. She turned to the people with her, who had tears in their eyes. She explained to me, "I have brain cancer, and this will be my touchstone. I will touch it for strength every time I leave the house. I will beat this!" Whenever I see that print, I believe she made it.

I talked with a woman whose husband of 55 years had recently passed away. She didn't know how to live without him, but she knew she owed it to him to live the best life she could. When she saw the artwork, *You didn't give me permission to be powerful. You empowered me so that I could find it for myself* she said it was representative of their life together. Her quiet dignity inspired me.

I noticed a young woman in my booth wiping away her tears. She grabbed a print and walked over to a man. He wrapped his arms around her and hugged her tight. She confided to me that she had previously been in an abusive relationship and still struggled with its impact on her life. That day she purchased *The echoes of my past will no longer haunt my future*. As she turned to leave, her companion bought *She found her voice and started becoming the person she always knew she could be*. When he handed it to her, they both cried...so did I.

CONTENTS

Section One
   Bravely Following Your Heart
      Value Sort 12
      Values Compass 19
      Explorations 23

Section Two
   Choosing The Moments
      Coloring Pages 33
      Explorations 41

Section Three
   Embrace Your Imperfections
      Authenticity Puzzle 51
      Explorations 59

Section Four
   Seeking A Balance
      Life Garden 69
      Explorations 75

Section Five
   I Can And I Will
      Inspirational Art 85
      Explorations 93

Examples 96
References 97
Recommendations 99
Resources 101

INTRODUCTION

In the past, we felt restricted, inadequate, and frustrated by self-doubt and self-criticism. Confronting our emotions allowed us to feel a sense of control. In this book, we share some of the practices that helped us. We wish you much joy and strength on your journey.

Each section has five parts: overview (Sneak Peek), narrative, personal reflections, hands-on activity (Power Moment) and questions for you to explore (Explorations).

Tips:
- ♥ We suggest reading the narrative first, where we explain each topic and give evidence for how it can be helpful in your life.
- ♥ Our reflections describe our personal experience with each topic, and how it has impacted our lives.
- ♥ We want you to experience the topics in the book, so we've included hands-on activities (Power Moments). These are for you to tear out, color on, glue, and otherwise make your own.
- ♥ Explorations are guiding journal questions where you can explore your reactions to the material.
- ♥ In the back is an appendix with even more resources that have helped us.

This book is yours. You can hide it in your room or display it proudly for all your guests. We hope you crease it, tear it, cut it up, and write all over it. The artwork was thoughtfully chosen to represent the theme of each section. You can remove the art as motivation or after you complete the chapter as a reminder of what you've learned (there's an overview of each section on the back). We've included paper for you to journal on and blank space for doodling. Make this journey your own!

SHE WAS *Brave* WHEN SHE FOLLOWED HER *Heart*

Sneak Peek

Theme - Bravely Following Your Heart
The standards we use to navigate our lives are called "values." Learning about your values can allow you to understand more about yourself and what drives you.

Power Moment - Values Sort
We provide a list of fifty words for you to cut out and sort. This activity is designed to help you discover your core values.

Explorations
Our culture often teaches us values. What values does your culture promote? How do you relate to these?

Many of our values are learned. What values did your family hold in high esteem?

List decisions you made in the last few days. What guided these choices? What role did your values play in your final decision?

BRAVELY FOLLOWING YOUR HEART

If someone were trying to decide between taking a high paying job that requires travel, or a lower paying job at home, how might they choose? If wealth, productiveness, and adventure were important to them, which job do you think they would take? What if they wanted stability, comfort, and leisure? Our choices are influenced by our beliefs - also known as values.

Values are the standards we use to navigate our lives. They can be a window to understanding ourselves and what drives our actions. Values influence how we see our relationship with others and allow us to know what we will, and won't, tolerate.[1] Since values are so important, it's worthwhile to consider how they are formed.

Our culture, our family, and our friends can instill values in us.[2] These often become societal norms. What happens when your beliefs don't fit with tradition? It can leave us disconnected, or feeling like an outsider.[3] While we may accept the values we are given, we can also create our own. Values are fluid and can shift throughout your life. Isn't that inspiring? If you don't like the values you have right now, make new ones!

It takes bravery and hard work to establish our own set of values and break away from what we've always known. It requires following your own path, listening to your heart, and knowing what's true to you. While discovering your values takes effort, it can be highly rewarding.

Determining your values will give you a better understanding of what motivates and inspires you. Recognizing your values set allows you to develop your internal navigation system. You can reference this, like a compass, to achieve your goals. The same way that following a map gets you to your destination faster, so can following your values.

Cassy's reflection:

The first time anyone asked me about my 'values,' I was in my early 20's at a career retreat. Honestly, I had no idea what they meant. After we did our values sorting activity, there was a lot of curiosity and discussion about our results (we were psychology students, after all). I felt proud of myself and intrigued by the results. It was as if this activity had given me a way to understand something that was hidden deep in my mind.

When I came home from the retreat, I encouraged all my friends to do a value sort. I wanted other people to experience the clarity and excitement I had felt when I learned the words to describe what meant so much to me. The next time I did a values sort, I was in graduate school. By this time, some of my values had shifted, and it was almost like meeting a brand new me.

I feel empowered and surprised every time I do this activity. Sorting your values gives you the opportunity to peek inside your mind, your role is to be willing to accept what you find there.

Tamara's reflection:

Family is a value I hold in high esteem. I love playing games, watching movies, enjoying lively conversation, and just spending time together as a family. When my daughters were young, I was self-employed, so I was able to arrange my schedule to be with them as much as possible. As they moved into their teen years, I took a job and lost much of that flexibility.

For the first time in fifteen years, my focus became my job and not my family. I felt torn between being a good wife, mother, and employee. Although I had enjoyed my work and the paycheck that came with it, I struggled with feeling inadequate in my personal life.

It wasn't until years later that I realized I was not living a values-driven life. If my values had been different, I might have been happier in my job. The past four years have been a work in progress. I quit my job, started a business, and am creating a life that holds value to me. I have seen the difference between living a life outside of my value system and living one within. There truly is a shift in how I view the world around me and how I view myself.

POWER MOMENT

Now that you have learned more about personal values, we ask that you bravely follow your heart and explore your own. On the following pages, we encourage you to examine your values set as well as those you have learned from society, family, and friends. As you do, consider if they resonate with the person you are today.

On the next two pages, you will find a list of fifty words. We compiled these so you can explore a variety of values (you may even see some that are outside of your everyday vocabulary!).

1) Get your scissors out! You'll need to cut the values list into fifty individual pieces.

2) For this next part, we like to set a timer for no more than three minutes. You'll want to move quick and listen to your gut as you sort the values into three categories (essential, important, irrelevant).

>   Essential - The 'I can't live without this in my life' values
>   Important - The 'I like it, but don't need it to survive' values
>   Irrelevant - The 'Not my cup of tea' values

3) Discard the 'irrelevant' words; you won't be using these anymore. Combine the 'essential' and 'important' piles, leaving you with one stack of values words.

4) Get ready for déjà vu...you'll once again sort your words into three categories (essential, important, irrelevant). Thoughtfully consider each value and don't set a timer. While all the words in these stacks are significant to you, your most closely held values should be in the 'essential' and 'important' piles.

5) At this step, your goal is to decide on your top twelve values. Use your 'essential' pile first, then supplement from your 'important' pile if necessary.

6) The final process will be to arrange your values in a hierarchy, with the most significant toward the top. Here are a few ways we have tried:
    Select #1 and #12 to reference as anchor points
    Pick out only the most significant and start at the top
    Start with your middle values and work outward
    Do another round of sorting

Congratulations on your hard work! You've isolated your value set. We will be referencing this in the next few activities.

VALUES COMPASS

Place your values on the compass provided. The largest point at the top of the page (your True North) will be your most important value. It will become the primary point in your internal navigation system and will always lead you home.

Position your second, third and fourth values on the larger points around the compass. Now you can place your remaining values (fifth, sixth, seventh, eighth) on the smaller points (example on page 96).

Reference this often - especially when you are making a decision!

FINDING IT FOR YOURSELF

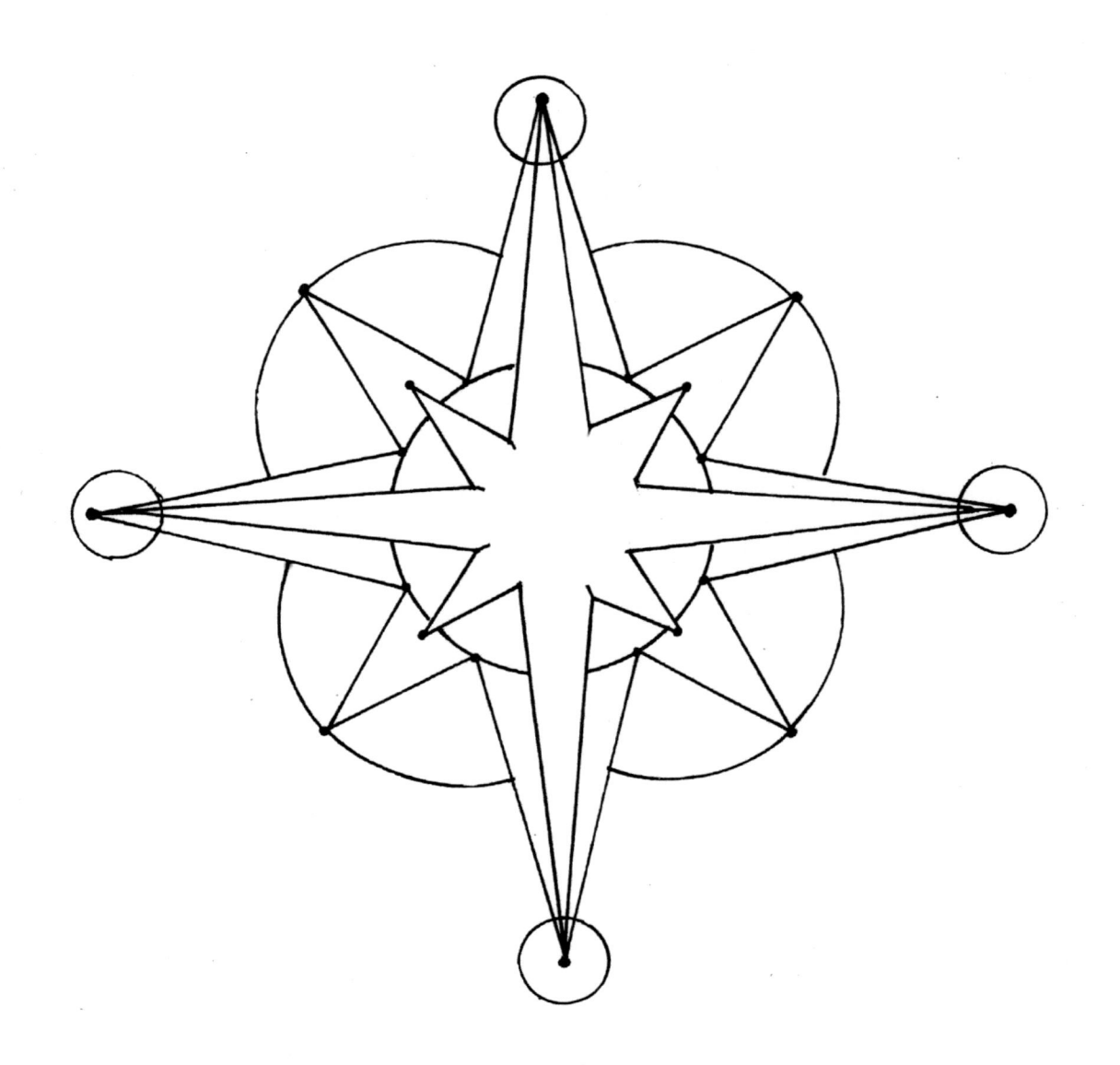

Our culture often teaches us values. What values does your culture promote? How do you relate to these?

Many of our values have been learned. What values did your family hold in high esteem?

_____

_____

_____

_____

_____

_____

_____

_____

_____

_____

List decisions you made in the last few days. What guided these choices? What role did your values play in your final decision?

_____

_____

_____

_____

_____

_____

_____

_____

_____

_____

_____

SHE chose the moments that would define her life

FINDING IT FOR YOURSELF

Sneak Peek

Theme - Choosing Your Moments
Our busy, repetitive lives lead us to spend a lot of time on autopilot. Staying focused on what is happening right now will help you be present and choose your moments.

Power Moment - Coloring Pages
We provide three coloring pages drawn just for this book. This activity is designed to help you focus on the present moment.

Explorations
What were your expectations when you started the coloring activity? Did anything about the experience surprise you?

How do you react when you have a few moments alone? Do you reach for your phone, or do you find it easy to sit with your thoughts? Set a timer for one minute and concentrate on your breathing and the sounds around you. Sometimes your mind can use a reboot - just like your computer! Write a few descriptive words about what it felt like to be present in the moment.

One of us loves to cook, and the other loves wine (guess who). Can you recall what the last meal you ate tasted like, or did you eat and run? At your next meal, concentrate on the experience of eating and drinking. Reflect on what it felt like to be mindful.

CHOOSING YOUR MOMENTS

Have you ever experienced 'highway hypnosis' – when you get in the car and drive a route so familiar that you don't remember driving?[4] Our thoughts can be so distracting that we experience amnesia behind the wheel! When we take a well-known road, our consciousness can split in two. One mind is automatically guiding us to our destination while the other thinks about what to do this weekend or relives an argument with a loved one. While we can do twice as much this way, we're only half present.[5]

Our busy, repetitive lives lead us to spend a lot of time on autopilot. We take the same route to work, eat at the same restaurants, and shop at the same stores. We fall into a pattern of making choices only when we're faced with them – like when the road to work is under construction, or our favorite grocery store is closed. Instead of reacting when we must, take an extra moment to choose thoughtfully. Making choices with intent can help us achieve our goals, advocate for our personal needs, and become more self-aware.[6]

When we can't act on auto-pilot and have to make choices, we can experience stress or other emotions that we like to avoid. Instead of staying busy and ignoring those feelings, we can check in and be honest about what is driving that emotion. Are we feeling motivated by kindness, hope, joy, or are we being influenced by guilt, worry, and fear? Acting in a way that is mindful can help us decide what to do or where to spend our energy with purpose.

Staying focused on what is happening right now will help you be present and choose your moments. Checking in with yourself isn't a new skill to learn, it's something you already do. Practicing mindfulness and proactive thinking allows you to feel more in control.[7] By recognizing why you are feeling or acting the way you are, you become the captain of your ship. Feeling in control of your experience is pretty empowering.

Cassy's reflection:

I have a lot of valuable skills. I cook fantastic Indian food, fold a shirt in under five seconds, and pick things up with my toes. Mindfulness is not in my wheelhouse. I like feeling busy, and if things slow down for too long, I've been known to manufacture problems where there are none. Case in point, one Spring Break I spent an entire afternoon stressing over how grimy the washing machine was and looking for solutions on the internet.

I think mindfulness is uniquely challenging for those of us with depression and anxiety. When my mind gets quiet, I have to face the actual problems that I've spent time avoiding. Real issues, like whether I'm happy and if I've made the right decisions in life and how I feel knowing that everyone I love will eventually die.

The first piece of good news is that mindfulness is an actual *skill*. That means that practicing it will improve it. The second bit of good news is that we can use that power to manage and cope with stressors, including depression and anxiety. Instead of channeling my energy into diversions, mindfulness lets me slow down and get to a place where I'm emotionally ready to confront my problems.

Tamara's reflection:

One day I realized that I was continually living my life on fast forward. It wasn't some earth-shattering awakening, but a slow cascade of moments that lead me to question the way I was focusing my life.

My husband and I were curled up in our favorite chairs enjoying a quiet evening. He grabbed us two candy bars from the kitchen (Almond Joy is my favorite). I realized I had eaten the entire candy bar without even knowing it. It was a sobering moment. I was lost in my mental to-do list and focusing on what I should get done, and not what I was doing.

I started to parallel the mindless eating of my Almond Joy bar to other things in my life. I recalled the numerous times I had spent at family outings thinking about what needed to get done and not what was happening right in front of me. Too many times I disregarded the moments of my life instead of truly absorbing them as they were being lived. Even to this day I feel a sense of loss for the moments I wasted.

For me, being mindful has a way of slowing me down. I become more deliberate with my actions. I feel the wind on my face and the pavement beneath my feet when I go for a walk. I listen intently to the sounds of nature and my beating heart. I feel more connected to the world around me when I concentrate on what is happening in the moment.

POWER MOMENT

On the following pages, you'll find three coloring sheets. While adult coloring has gained popularity in the last three years, there is good evidence that it's more than just a trend. Coloring helps children relax and concentrate, which allows them to take control of their emotions.[8] There are similar benefits for teens and adults.[9]

Artmaking has been considered a viable form of therapy for many years, but coloring has a different advantage.[10] Rather than generating your own art, coloring provides structure and allows you to follow a complex pattern. In other words, coloring doesn't require you to create out of thin air. Instead, it directs your attention toward completing a task. Like meditation, coloring requires you to focus on the present moment and can bring about improved mindfulness.[11]

The following coloring pages were drawn just for this book. They range in complexity and subject matter, so explore which you enjoy the most. Make this activity your own by using markers, colored pencils, crayons, or watercolors to fill in the designs. Bonus tip: we like to play our favorite music in the background while we color!

We'd love to see what you've created. Snap a picture and share it on social media (use #WomensPowerMoment), our website, or send us an email!

Finding it for yourself

FINDING IT FOR YOURSELF

FINDING IT FOR YOURSELF

FINDING IT FOR YOURSELF

What were your expectations when you started the coloring activity? Did anything about the experience surprise you?

How do you react when you have a few moments alone? Do you reach for your phone, or do you find it easy to sit with your thoughts? Set a timer for one minute and concentrate on your breathing and the sounds around you. Sometimes your mind can use a reboot - just like your computer! Write a few descriptive words about what it felt like to be present in the moment.

_____

_____

_____

_____

_____

_____

_____

_____

_____

One of us loves to cook, and the other loves wine (guess who). Can you recall what the last meal you ate tasted like, or did you eat and run? At your next meal, concentrate on the experience of eating and drinking. Reflect on what it felt like to be mindful.

embrace your imperfections

Sneak Peek

Theme - Embrace Your Imperfections
When we compare our beginnings to others crowning achievements, we forget they failed along the way. Everyone has obstacles and setbacks. Reminding ourselves of this can help us to feel less alone and shameful about our faults and failures.

Power Moment - Personal Puzzle
We provide twelve puzzle pieces for you to write on and cut out. This activity lets you practice loving your authentic self.

Explorations
Imagine you're having a conversation with a close friend. They reveal that they're feeling ashamed due to a recent mistake. How would you respond? Write down a few ways that you would support them.

Now, imagine you're feeling ashamed due to a recent mistake. How do you respond? Revisit your answer to the previous journal prompt. How does your compassion for others compare to compassion for yourself?

Brainstorm a word or motto which prompts you to practice self-compassion. The next time your inner voice starts to be unkind, use this motto to remind yourself to stop and reflect. What other strategies do you have for being proactively self-compassionate?

EMBRACE YOUR IMPERFECTIONS

We all have a little voice in our head that reminds us to grab lettuce at the store or to set the alarm clock. But what happens when that little voice, the voice we so often trust, turns against us? It starts to place judgment on our actions, and we might even believe what it tells us. That voice may convince us that we're not smart enough, pretty enough, or worthy enough. In these times, we can practice self-compassion.[12]

When we feel inadequate or doubtful of ourselves, compassion allows us to react to those feelings without judgment or avoidance.[13] People who face negative feelings with kindness and sensitivity report decreased anxiety, decreased depression, and a more positive outlook on life than those who aren't practicing self-compassion.[14]

The times we need compassion the most are often the times we provide it the least. Being kind to ourselves is more comfortable when we meet our expectations and live up to our standards. When we let ourselves down or fall short of our goals, we might react with self-criticism. Everyone wants to know if our performance measures up – did we do worse than others? Better? About the same? It's one thing to get information about how we did. It's another to judge ourselves based on that. When we compare our beginnings to others crowning achievements, we forget that they failed along the way.

Most people don't talk about the struggles they've experienced, but we have a front row seat to watch our own mistakes. Everyone has obstacles and setbacks. Reminding ourselves of this can help us to feel less alone and shameful about our faults and failures.[15] Even your role models have felt isolated, regretful, and defeated.

Learning to accept others as flawed and messy people can help shape your relationship with yourself. Extend others warmth and understanding. You will be more compassionate toward yourself when you remember that you are a good, caring, kind, human being while also being occasionally careless, unproductive, or too sensitive. Try having a relationship with your whole self, rather than hiding or ignoring the imperfect parts. A lousy choice or failure doesn't make you any less worthy.

Cassy's reflection:

"Who are you telling off?" my boyfriend asked. I was driving us home, but he'd been watching me silently frown and gesture to myself behind the wheel. I'd been reliving a confrontation I'd had earlier in the day with a coworker. I had bristled at one of her comments and wanted to speak up and defend myself clearly and articulately…instead, I'd stayed quiet and meekly walked away.

Now, hours later, I found myself in the car admitting my weakness to my boyfriend. "Now I can think of exactly what I should have said to her. I'm timid. I'm just bad at asserting myself." He listened as I poured out my insecurities and punished myself for failing. After a few minutes, he stopped me and put things into perspective. He reminded me of times when I've been brave, and how strong I can be when I feel passionate about something.

What prevented me from saying those words to myself? I've been putting extra work into being self-compassionate when I feel guilty or overwhelmed. Somehow I forget to acknowledge all the stressors in my life, and instead feel weak for not being able to handle it all. That's one of my emotional blind spots. Recognizing these is helping me to take steps toward being gentle with myself.

Tamara's reflection:

Of all the concepts included in our book, self-compassion is what I struggle with the most. I often listen to the little voice in my head that points out my short-comings and failures. The voice that tells me I'm not good enough, pretty enough, successful enough. It's the mean girl!

I am now learning to accept my "mean girl" voice and counter her with words of my own. I find I can listen objectively and quiet her response. I have become less afraid of what others think and more concerned with finding my inner peace. We all have baggage that we carry with us. Appearance and acceptance have always been mine.

In the past, I placed judgment on others based on what they wore, how they looked, how normative they appeared. When I judged others by these factors, I judged myself too. As I became less judgmental of others, I became less critical of myself.

I still struggle with self image issues and don't like having my picture taken. I find it difficult to be the center of attention. I recognize my short comings in these areas and am compassionately working towards self-acceptance.

POWER MOMENT

This activity will let you view your authentic self holistically.

What aspects of yourself do you admire? In the spaces below, write a list of nine traits or qualities that you appreciate about yourself. Use a mix of physical, mental, and personality traits.

What aspects of yourself do you struggle to love? In the remaining three spaces, write three traits or qualities that you feel limited by. Again, use a mix of physical, mental, and personality traits.

_____   _____   _____

_____   _____   _____

_____   _____   _____

_____   _____   _____

On the following pages, you will find twelve puzzle pieces. Cut them out and write one trait on each piece. Now, you can put your puzzle together! You can't finish the puzzle if you only use some of the pieces - all of them come together to make a unique, beautiful image. Our authentic self is more than just the things we like, we're made of our strengths *and* our limitations.

FINDING IT FOR YOURSELF

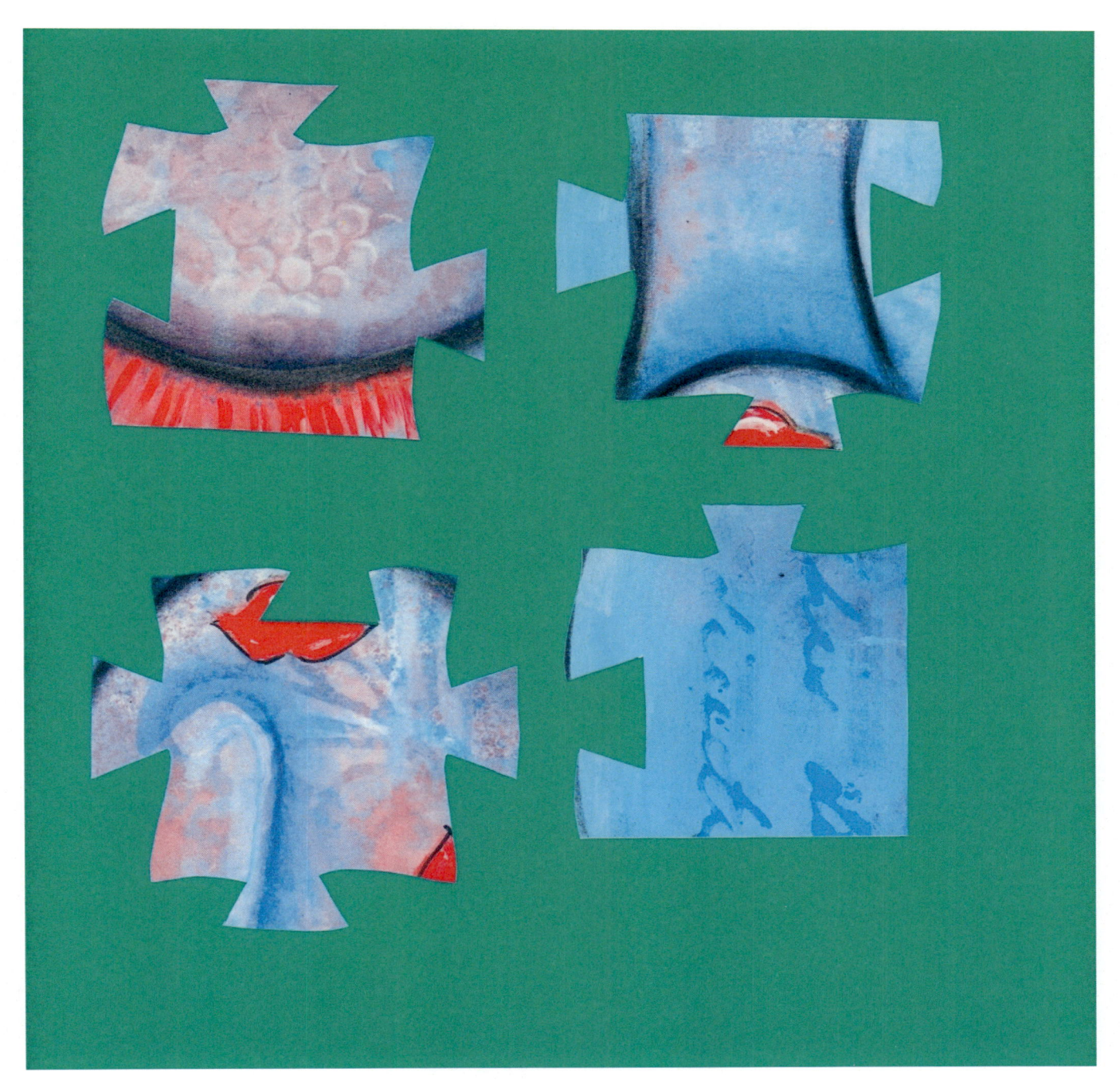

Finding it for yourself

FINDING IT FOR YOURSELF

Imagine you're having a conversation with a close friend. They reveal that they're feeling ashamed due to a recent mistake. How would you respond? Write down a few ways that you would support them.

_____

_____

_____

_____

_____

_____

_____

_____

_____

Now, imagine *you're* feeling ashamed due to a recent mistake. How do you respond? Revisit your answer to the previous journal prompt. How does your compassion for others compare to compassion for yourself?

_____

_____

_____

_____

_____

_____

_____

_____

_____

_____

Brainstorm a word or motto which prompts you to practice self-compassion. The next time your inner voice starts to be unkind, use this motto to remind yourself to stop and reflect. What other strategies do you have for being proactively self-compassionate?

I give myself permission to seek a balanced life

FINDING IT FOR YOURSELF

Sneak Peek

Theme - Seeking A Balanced Life
While you may strive to live an enlightened, mindful, nurtured, values-driven life, it's hard to do it all! Developing balance can help you to manage stress, prevent burnout, and become aware of your vulnerabilities.

Power Moment - Personal Garden
We provide an activity for you to visualize the balance in your life by cutting out and planting flowers. You can maintain your garden with pruning shears, water, and fertilizer.

Explorations
Do you feel balanced and in control today? If not, did the garden activity reveal anything that needed re-balancing?

Earlier we discussed the benefits of being proactive. Use this space to brainstorm a few actions that give you power over your day. For instance, we like to create lists and prioritize them. We also find value in setting and reaching small goals. If we can do one thing we set our minds to, we prove that we can hold ourselves accountable.

Living a balanced life requires that we advocate for our needs. Write about a time you successfully advocated for yourself. What inspired you to do so?

SEEKING A BALANCED LIFE

Attention is like a spotlight, because it highlights what we are focused on.[16] We often shine that spotlight on achievements in the future while forgetting to light the present. While it is important to achieve goals, it also matters how we navigate the journey to those goals. Developing balance can help you manage stress, prevent burnout, and become aware of your vulnerabilities.

Self-care is vital to our wellbeing, yet we often fail to practice it. Balancing a variety of areas in our lives – physical, psychological, emotional, spiritual, relationships, you name it – may be challenging. When we neglect one of these areas, we are susceptible to burnout.[17] We can call on friends and family to help uplift us, but no social support network knows you as well as you know yourself. In that way, self-care draws on both self-awareness and mindfulness.

How do we raise ourselves up? You may have heard of self-care as bubble baths and yoga classes, but it's more than just doing things that feel good. It's also about setting ourselves up for success. Self-care can mean advocating in our own best interest by saying no to new commitments or by getting our taxes done on time, so we're not stressed about April 15th.

It can be holding ourselves accountable to a plan of action so that we mitigate stressors in our life. For instance, if we're stressed about finances we may feel bad about overspending. Remorse may send us to the mall where we spend even more. In this case, self-care may mean following a budget to pay down debt. As you practice self-awareness, you'll be able to gauge your energy and know when to re-balance your life with self-care. This process can help you feel more connected to yourself, which enables you to be aware of your needs, which you can then address.[18] What a great feedback loop!

Cassy's reflection:

I know the research on benefits of self-care. You'd think that someone who knows how important it is would be great at keeping their life in balance. Paradoxically, feeling as if it's something I should do can make it feel like a skipped day at the gym.

It's hard to prioritize self-care when I view it as yet another thing on my to-do list. On those days, it helps me to think of self-care as a tool rather than an action. Self-care can help me be more efficient and less stressed, it's not something I have to accomplish to check it off my list. I found the garden activity to be beneficial – it's a way to visualize all the things in life that we have to keep balanced.

Some of my favorite forms of self-care are quick and have a good return-on-investment. Dance to your favorite song in the kitchen, get rid of a to-do list lurker (the things that seem to always stay on your list), spend a few minutes reducing the people you follow on social media, stretch, lay in the sun, clean out your inbox, go out of your way to strike up a conversation with a stranger, take a drive.

Tamara's reflection:

I know I need self-care when I have difficulty sleeping, overeat, become irritable, and the simple joys of life become mundane. That's when I know I need to decompress.

I shamelessly reschedule meetings and appointments. I look at my to-do list and arrange them in a hierarchy. I focus my attention on the items that need doing, even if I don't want to do them (taxes, bookkeeping, etc.). Typically these are the items that cause me the most stress. If I can get at least one of these crossed off my list, I start to feel the pressure subside.

Self-care for me isn't a bubble bath or spa day. It's holding myself accountable for the actions I need to take - whether it's having a heart-to-heart with my husband or getting my homework done (I'm completing my bachelors in HR management at the age of 60). It's when I practice self-care, in all its capacity, that I can begin to live a more balanced life. Of course, sometimes self-care means I open my favorite bottle of wine and just enjoy the pleasure of sipping it slowly. I put my favorite music on and let my mind wander.

POWER MOMENT

Now that you know the importance of self-care, we have an activity to help you visualize your life balance (example on page 96). We brainstormed several life areas, which you will find below. Spend a moment appreciating how many roles you play and how many areas of your life there are – no wonder keeping it balanced is hard!

Stress, Nutrition, Friends, Physical fitness, Leisure, Family, Love life, Social, Spiritual, Work, School, Recreation, Adventure, Psychological, Emotional, Learning, Financial, Community

1) Circle five life areas that you would like to reflect on. You can use the list above or write in your own.

2) On the following pages, you will find your personal garden and a sheet of gardening materials. To prepare for this activity, cut your flowers, fertilizer, water, and pruners into individual pieces (we provided guidelines since some of us experience 'crooked scissor syndrome'). On your garden page, write the five life areas you circled above into the header of each garden row.

3) Now, consider each of these life areas. How much energy do you put in, and how much accomplishment are you getting out? The flowers represent 'blooming,' to signify how much each area is flourishing. For example, if you have dedicated a lot of time to budgeting and paying off debt lately, your 'finances' row may have lots of flowers. Decide how full each row should be and place the flowers accordingly. Hint: don't fill any row to the brim, you'll need some spare room for 'maintenance' (step 5). Glue or tape the flowers in place once you are satisfied with their arrangement.

4) Take a look at your handiwork. Are you satisfied with the balance in your garden? Are certain rows blooming more than others? For instance, our leisure row had a lot of blossoms, but our school row was pretty scarce…time for some self-care to balance things out!

5) Use the pruning shears, water, and fertilizer to maintain your garden. Place pruning shears on the areas that you'd like to spend less energy on (for us, this was 'leisure). Use water on the areas you want to feed (for us, this was 'school'). If you have rows that look particularly deprived, dump some fertilizer on them! Glue or tape these in place once you are satisfied with their arrangement.

Great work! You've finished your personal garden. We'll ask you to reflect on it during the next few activities.

FINDING IT FOR YOURSELF

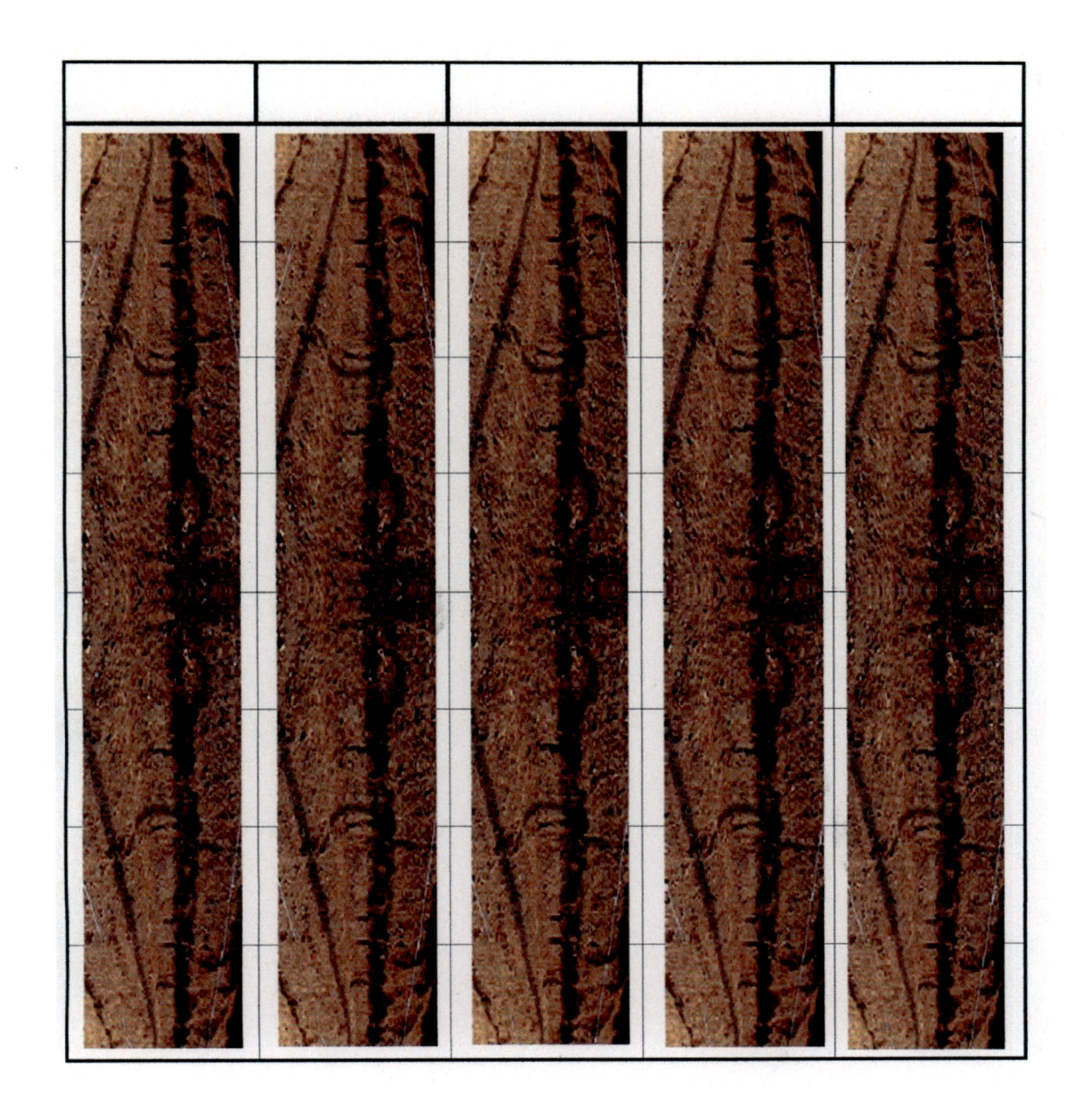

FINDING IT FOR YOURSELF

Do you feel balanced and in control today? If not, did the garden activity reveal anything that needed re-balancing?

_____
_____
_____
_____
_____
_____
_____
_____
_____

Earlier we discussed the benefits of being proactive. Use this space to brainstorm a few actions that give you power over your day. For instance, we like to create lists and prioritize them. We also find value in setting and reaching small goals. If we can do one thing we set our minds to, we prove that we can hold ourselves accountable.

_____

_____

_____

_____

_____

_____

_____

_____

_____

_____

Living a balanced life requires that we advocate for our needs. Write about a time you successfully advocated for yourself. What inspired you to do so?

_____

_____

_____

_____

_____

_____

_____

_____

_____

_____

I can

and I will.

Just watch me.

FINDING IT FOR YOURSELF

Sneak Peek

Theme - I Can And I Will
Did you know you can be inspired *by* something and you can be inspired *to* something? Being inspired *by* something can uplift us, while being inspired *to* something drives us to action.

Power Moment - Inspirational Art
We designed three pieces of art for you to enhance with your own quote. You will make your own inspirational touchstones!

Explorations
Write about things you are inspired *by*. What do they have in common? What are your inspirations leading you toward?

What are things you are inspired *to*? Describe a few small steps that you can take. How do you feel when you are inspired *to* - excited, overwhelmed, fearful, hopeful?

Take action to be inspired. For example, we like to create, connect with likeminded others, take classes, go for a walk in nature, look at the stars, or bake. Journal about your experience.

I CAN AND I WILL

How do you feel when you are inspired? While we may enjoy the rush of creativity and encouragement that comes with inspiration, it reaches far beyond ourselves. Inspiration changes not only individuals but also societies.[19] In February of 2004, Mark Zuckerberg had the idea to create Facebook. That website changed his life, and also how people all across the world connect with one another. That's a pretty powerful idea!

While researching this topic, we were surprised to learn there are different forms of inspiration. For example, we can be inspired *by* something, or we can be inspired *to* something. When we think about people who inspire us, we are being inspired *by*. The ancient Greeks called them muses, but they can also be our idols, role models, or family members. We can be inspired *by* stories of average people who have overcome extraordinary obstacles, defied expectations, or strayed from the norm. Thinking about their bravery and confidence may encourage us to take action, which is when we are inspired *to*.

You may be inspired *to* confront something you've been avoiding, create a piece of art, or make a new goal for yourself. Unique and interesting doors inspire me. One door, in particular, is located on the grounds of Trinity College in Ireland. I found this door so inspiring that I used it in a painting. I was inspired *by* the door *to* create a piece of artwork.

Inspiration has the power to change us by giving us an appreciation for new and better possibilities.[19] Changing takes bravery. Whether we're inspired *by* or *to* something, embracing inspiration gives us confidence. Favorite quotes can awaken hope and strength, which can power us through difficult times. One look at Pinterest tells you there are many things people are inspired *by*. We may collect these inspirations until one day we find ourselves being inspired *to* action. Taking that step will lead to failures, victories, and triumphs. None of those things are possible until you try. You can, and we know you will.

Cassy's reflection:

Occasionally, I feel kind of stale. I start to get drained and notice my defenses dropping low enough for self-doubt and hesitancy to grow. Inevitably, decisions that were once simple and straightforward become challenging. I question my judgment and talents. Can I do this? Should I?

I need some inspiration to push past my fears and doubts so that I can achieve the things I value so much. In our scariest moments, inspiration can be the most valuable. I feel inspired when I can put my life into perspective. The things I'm afraid of seem trivial in comparison to the height of the mountains and the vastness of the stars.

I also get inspired when I think of my role models and their achievements. Each of these people had a day when they didn't know how to handle the challenges in front of them. They have overcome childhood trauma, mental illness, physical handicaps, social rejection, poverty, and they're still making their way in the world. I find a lot of strength in being inspired by others' stories. It helps me recognize that others have faced incredible odds and persevered. Remembering this makes taking a leap feel a little less scary, and a lot more rewarding.

Tamara's reflection:

As a mother of two daughters, I have realized that by living my dream, I may be inspiring my girls to follow theirs. We give permission to others in our life to pursue their passion when they see us following ours. When we reach for a larger life, we open the possibilities to others. We mustn't live small because we are too afraid to live large. We must live large because it's in us to do so.

I have begun to realize the power of sharing our stories and how it impacts others. I have had many customers who have asked how I started my business. When I tell them my story, they inevitably ask, "how did you know what to do" or "how did you know you would succeed"? The truth is, I didn't know what I would do or that I would succeed. It was intimidating and inspiring all at once.

It's been five years now and I still find myself over thinking every decision and doubting my abilities. It can be isolating and at times incapacitating. I have worked hard to overcome the voice of doubt in my head and to create a life that I find inspiring. When I hear others say I inspire them, I find it humbling and satisfying. Others have inspired me, and it's nice to know that maybe I am returning the favor. It comes full circle, and I am good with that.

POWER MOMENT

Here you'll find three pieces of artwork for you to enhance using a quote that you choose. Take a few minutes to look at each one. What quote, words, or phrase does each piece provoke?

Now you can remove the artwork and add your own words - we like using a few different methods:
- ♥ Handwrite or draw on the artwork itself.
- ♥ Type your quote, customize it with your favorite font or colors, and print it. Then you can cut out the words and glue them to the piece.
- ♥ Use both methods - handwrite your quote on a piece of paper and then glue it to your artwork.

You just made an inspirational touchstone! Display it somewhere you can reference it often - we have them in our office, bathroom, and on the refrigerator. You can even add a frame and hang it on your wall!

We'd love to see what you've created. Snap a picture and share it on social media (use #WomensPowerMoment), our website, or send us an email!

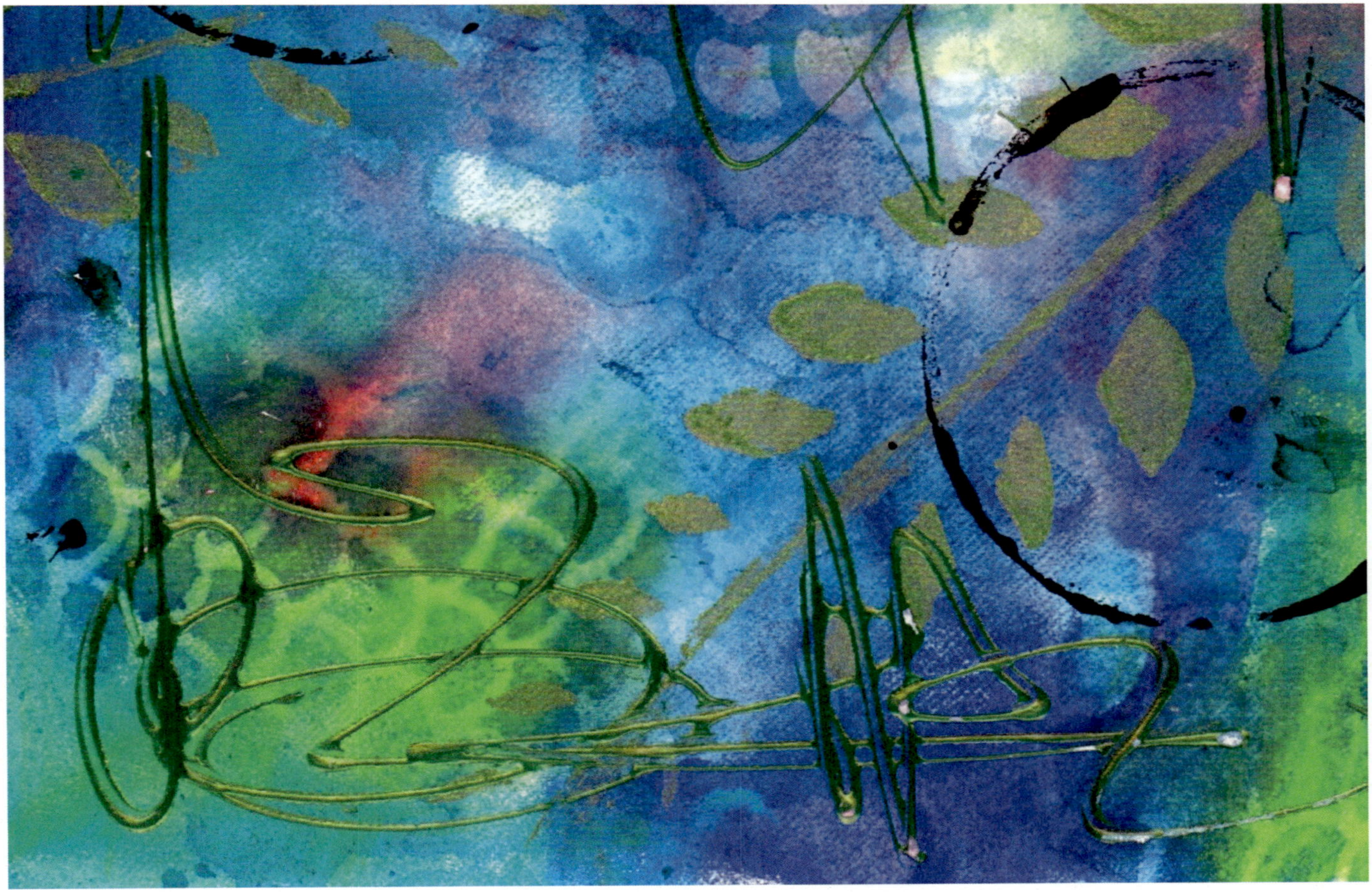

FINDING IT FOR YOURSELF

FINDING IT FOR YOURSELF

Write about things you are inspired *by*. What do they have in common? What are your inspirations leading you toward?

What are things you are inspired *to*? Describe a few small steps that you can take. How do you feel when you are inspired *to* - excited, overwhelmed, fearful, hopeful?

Take action to be inspired. For example, we like to create, connect with likeminded others, take classes, go for a walk in nature, look at the stars, or bake. Journal about your experience.

EXAMPLES

Personal Values Compass

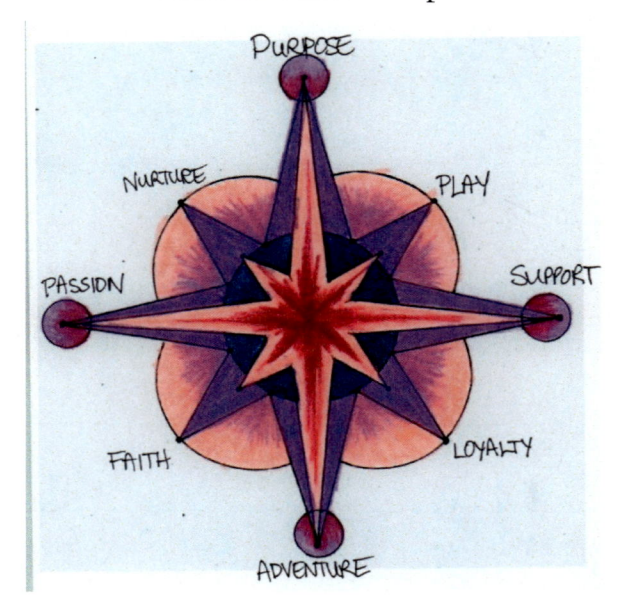

Self-Care Garden

FINDING IT FOR YOURSELF

REFERENCES

1. Roccas, S., Sagiv, L., Schwartz, S. H., & Knafo, A. (2002). The big five personality factors and personal values. *Personality and social psychology bulletin*, *28*(6), 789-801.

2. Schwartz, S. H. (1994). Are there universal aspects in the structure and contents of human values?. *Journal of social issues*, *50*(4), 19-45.

3. Roccas, S., Sagiv, L., Schwartz, S. H., & Knafo, A. (2002). The big five personality factors and personal values. *Personality and social psychology bulletin*, *28*(6), 789-801.

4. Corbett, K. (2017, January). Mindfulness and Its Impact on Health and Safety. In *ASSE Professional Development Conference and Exposition*. American Society of Safety Engineers.

5. Lubbe, R. H. J., Kleine, E., Schreurs, K., & Bohlmeijer, E. T. (2015). Mindfulness training increases the efficiency of attentional orienting: an examination with lateralized eeg power spectra. *Psychophysiology*, *52*(Suppl. 1), 73.

6. Greeson, J. M., Toohey, M. J., & Pearce, M. J. (2015). An adapted, four-week mind–body skills group for medical students: Reducing stress, increasing mindfulness, and enhancing self-care. *Explore: The Journal of Science and Healing*, *11*(3), 186-192.

7. Campos, D., Cebolla, A., Quero, S., Bretón-López, J., Botella, C., Soler, J., ... & Baños, R. M. (2016). Meditation and happiness: Mindfulness and self-compassion may mediate the meditation–happiness relationship. *Personality and Individual Differences*, *93*, 80-85.

8. Plummer, D. (2012). *Focusing and calming games for children: Mindfulness strategies and activities to help children to relax, concentrate and take control*. Jessica Kingsley Publishers.

9. Flett, J. A. M., Lie, C., Riordan, B. C., Thompson, L. M., Conner, T. S., & Hayne, H. (2017). Sharpen Your Pencils: Preliminary Evidence that Adult Coloring Reduces Depressive Symptoms and Anxiety. *Creativity Research Journal*, *29*(4), 409-416.

10. Curry, N. A., & Kasser, T. (2005). Can coloring mandalas reduce anxiety?. *Art Therapy*, *22*(2), 81-85.

11. K. Fitzpatrick, "Why adult coloring books are good for you," CNN, 1 August 2017. [Online]. Available: https://www.cnn.com/2016/01/06/health/adult-coloring-books-popularity-mental-health/index.html.

12. Neff, K. (2003). Self-compassion: An alternative conceptualization of a healthy attitude toward oneself. *Self and identity*, *2*(2), 85-101.

13. Wispé, L. (1991). *The psychology of sympathy*. Springer Science & Business Media.

14. Neff, K. D., & Vonk, R. (2009). Self-compassion versus global self-esteem: Two different ways of relating to oneself. *Journal of personality*, *77*(1), 23-50.

15. Neff, K. D., Hsieh, Y. P., & Dejitterat, K. (2005). Self-compassion, achievement goals, and coping with academic failure. *Self and identity*, *4*(3), 263-287.

16. Pashler, H. (Ed.). (2016). *Attention*. Psychology Press.

17. Skovholt, T. M., & Trotter-Mathison, M. (2014). *The resilient practitioner: Burnout prevention and self-care strategies for counselors, therapists, teachers, and health professionals*. Routledge.

18. Richards, K., Campenni, C., & Muse-Burke, J. (2010). Self-care and well-being in mental health professionals: The mediating effects of self-awareness and mindfulness. *Journal of Mental Health Counseling*, *32*(3), 247-264.

19. Baas, M., Nijstad, B. A., & De Dreu, C. K. (2015). "The cognitive, emotional and neural correlates of creativity". *Frontiers in human neuroscience*, *9*.

RECOMMENDATIONS

TEDTalks
- Frank Warren - Half A Million Secrets
- Shawn Achor - The Happy Secret To Better Work
- Brene Brown – The Power of Vulnerability

Authors
- Brene Brown – researcher who studies courage, vulnerability, shame, and empathy
- Cheryl Strayed – feminist memoirist
- Mary Roach – popular science humorist
- Roxane Gay – feminist memoirist

Apps
- Simple Habit – a library of meditation exercises to promote mindfulness
- Habitica – turn your to-do list into a game, tools to stay motivated and organized
- Words With Friends – connect with others and play word games
- Wordscapes – brain teasers using a crossword format
- Monkeywrench – quiz game with hidden words

Books
- Mystery of Making It – guide to living as an artist
- Big Magic – inspiration and motivation about the creative process
- Zenspirations – techniques for patterning
- Grit: The power and passion of perseverance – how character and effort influence outcomes
- Superbetter: The power of living gamefully – scientific research on resilience
- The Marshmallow Test – how self-control can help us overcome challenges
- The Happiness Trap: How to stop struggling and start living – values and mindfulness guide

Websites
- wildwomansisterhood.com – authentic feminist living
- donothingfor2minutes.com – relaxing mindfulness exercise
- rainymood.com – peaceful background noise
- thequietplaceproject.com/thequietplace - relaxing mindfulness exercise
- postsecret.com – community art project where people share secrets anonymously

RESOURCES

adaa.org
Resources on depression and anxiety for individuals and their loved ones

apa.org/helpcenter
Resources, support, and education for mental health

crisiscallcenter.org
Emotional support for those seeking help and information
1-800-273-8255 (all-hours crisis hotline)

hazeldenbettyford.org
Resources on addiction for individuals and their loved ones
1-866-297-4728

rainn.org
Resources and support for survivors of sexual assault
1-800-656-4673

Made in the USA
Lexington, KY
14 February 2018